THIS RAINDROP

Has a Billion Stories to Tell

Written by Linda Ragsdale
Illustrated by Srimalie Bassani

A raindrop has billions of stories to tell.
In fact, THIS raindrop has been here since time began!

This tiny drop could be the same drip once flipped off the tip of a pterodactyl's wing.

This drop could have plopped on the top of a T. rex or been tossed from the locks of a meandering mammoth.

Why, this drop could have ROARED in the crash of the first ocean wave.

Maybe this drip shifted sediment
that sculpted spectacular canyons and caverns.

This raindrop may have tippy-tapped on rooftops in cities and suburbs all over the world.

It might have tumbled off a towering ledge and been whisked away in a whooshing waterfall.

Maybe it hovered in fluffy clouds
stuffed with precipitation
in anticipation of a place to rain down.

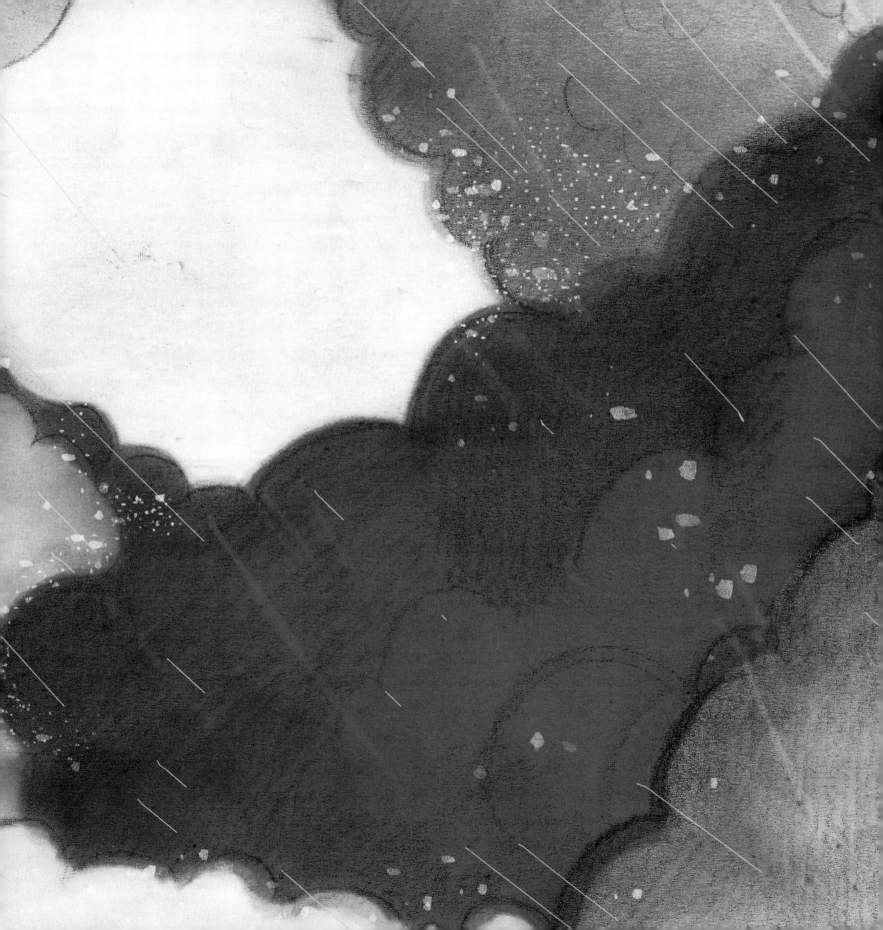

Perhaps it draped over peaks and pikes on parts of the planet unknown.

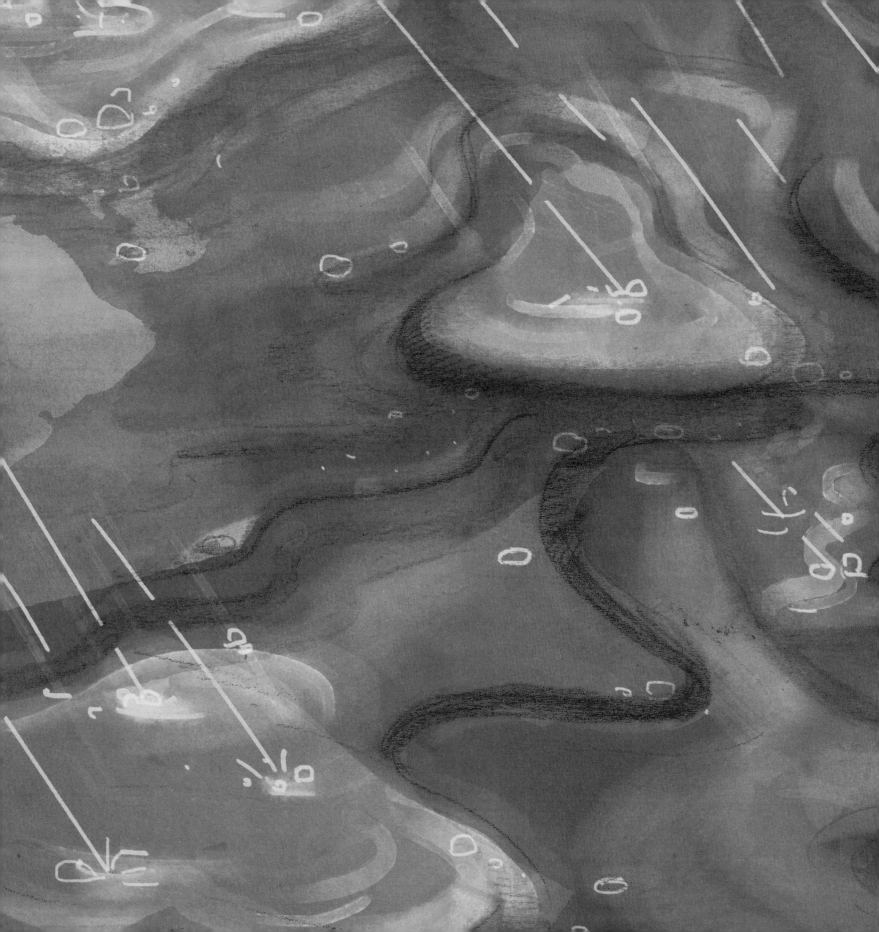

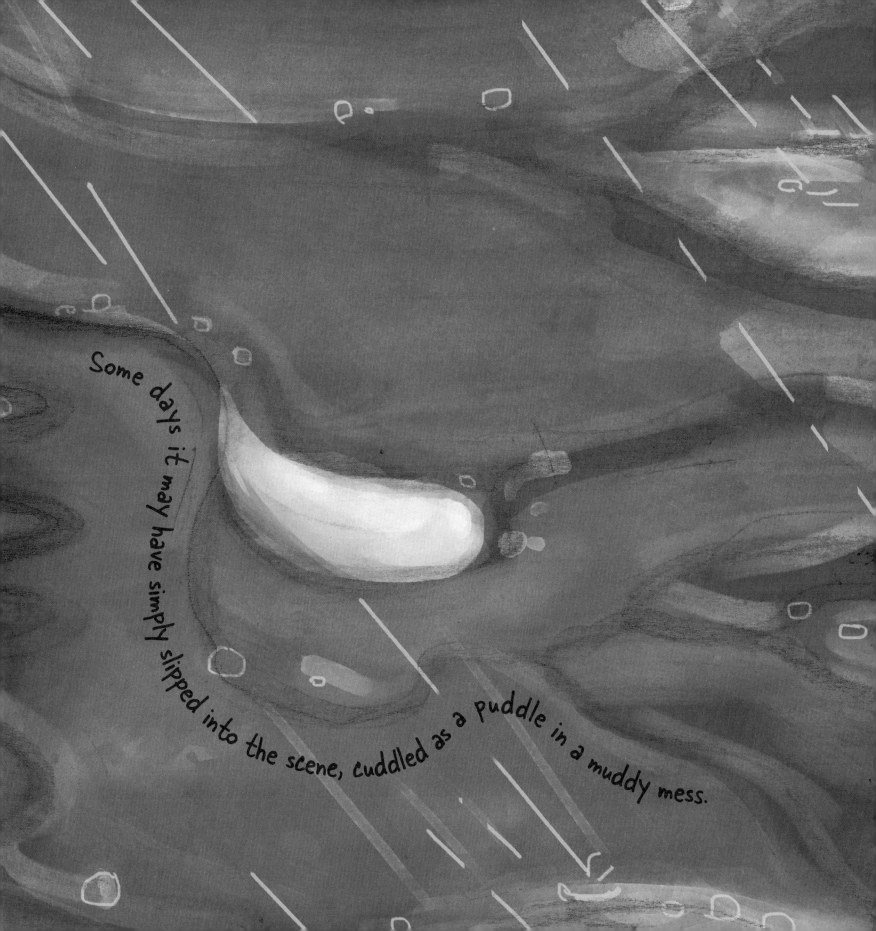

Some days it may have simply slipped into the scene, cuddled as a puddle in a muddy mess.

This drip is a master of mysteries!
Its magical molecules morph into thin air
then shape-shift back into something new,
like a single drop of dew in the morning.

Why, water has so many stories to spill!
From shore to shore,
it has shipped poets and pirates,
kings and queens,
astronauts, adventurers,
friends, fishermen,
sailors, soldiers, and seekers.

Water is a witness to the wonders of the world.

It is a source that flows in the oceans, air, and atmosphere.

It is a home and habitat for furry and finned friends.

It runs in rivers and veins, through bodies of land,

and through limbs and leaves of people and plants of all kinds!

Raindrops are fully versed
in the sagas and secrets
of travelers throughout time.
They connect everything
from then to now.

Next time a raindrop falls, catch it.
Look.
Listen.
Imagine.

It has billions of stories to tell.

It's incredible to think about just how long water has been on this big, blue planet of ours. Some scientists believe asteroids brought water to Earth millions of years ago, while others believe water has been here for billions of years, since our planet was formed. No matter when water came to Earth, one thing that's certain is that we've been recycling and reusing the water we have since its first days on our planet, as evidenced by the water cycle. This closed cycle shows how water exists in various forms throughout its lifetime but never truly goes away. This is why water has so many stories to tell!

WATER CYCLE

To understand how the same water has been on Earth for millions of years, it helps to understand the water cycle.

First, the water in oceans, lakes, ponds, rivers, and even puddles, changes from a liquid to a gas as it is heated by the sun. This gas rises into the atmosphere in a process called **EVAPORATION**.

As the water evaporates into the air, it cools down and forms clouds. This is called **CONDENSATION**.

When clouds get too heavy with condensed water, the water falls back to Earth. This process is called **PRECIPITATION**, which is more commonly known as rain, snow, sleet, or hail.

As the water falls to Earth, it may land back where it came from in bodies of water such as ponds, rivers, or oceans. It may also land on grass, roads, or soil, where it will soak into the earth and be used by plants to grow or animals to drink. It could also run off the land and into the nearest body of water. This process is called **COLLECTION**. Once the water has collected, it is warmed by the sun and starts to evaporate and the cycle begins again.

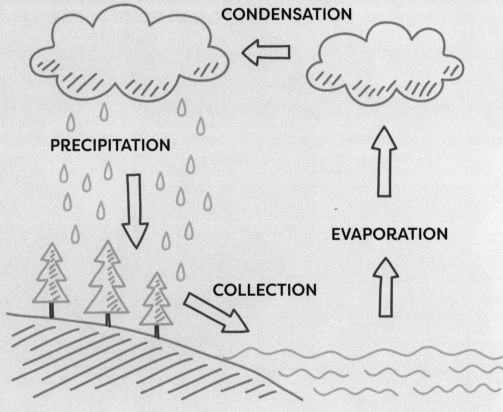

WATER CONSERVATION

As Earth's water has been moving through the water cycle for millions of years, our planet has changed a lot. From the days of dinosaurs to our present population of over *seven billion people*, Earth has depended on the same water supply.

Taking care of the water on Earth is important for every living creature. As the human population has grown, we have not always paid attention to keeping our water supply clean. The good news is many people around the world are realizing the need to protect the water we have. There are many organizations working on both cleaning up and protecting the world's water supply while other groups work to make sure all people on Earth have access to safe and clean water. There are many ways for you to participate in conserving water.

What can you do? Be water wise!
1. Turn off the water while you are brushing your teeth or washing your hands. You don't need to keep it running while you are scrubbing.
2. Save your laundry so you wash big loads all at once and only put dirty clothes in the laundry.
3. Reuse your shower water. Bring a bucket in the shower with you to catch the clean water as it runs down and use it for cleaning or to water house plants.
4. Put a bucket outside to capture the rainwater and use that to water your garden.
5. Learn more about water conservation and how other people in the world are affected by our limited water supply.

WORLD OCEANS DAY

Another way to participate is to celebrate World Oceans Day on June 8. People around the world join together each year to honor the oceans of the world, and now you can too!

To find out how you can get involved, visit their website at www.worldoceansday.org.

FURTHER READING

Hollyer, Beatrice. *Our World of Water: Children and Water Around the World*. New York, NY: Henry Holt and Company, 2008.

Dakers, Diane. *Earth's Water Cycle*. New York, NY: Crabtree Publishing Company, 2015.

Olien, Rebecca. *The Water Cycle at Work*. North Mankato, MN: Capstone Press, 2016.

Gallant, Roy A. *Water*. Kaleidoscope. Tarrytown, NY: Marshall Cavendish Corporation, 2001.

Kegley, David E. *Where Does Rain Come From?* New York, NY: The Rosen Publishing Group, 2002.

Simon, Seymour. *Water*. New York, NY: HarperCollins, 2017.

To learn even more about precipitation and the life of water, visit http://www.flowerpotpress.com/thisraindrop to find links to more resources and online content.

In an effort to improve our world and in collaboration with Trees for the Future (TREES), a tree will be planted for every book purchased. Our plant a tree partnership is a way for us to assist TREES in their efforts to heal the environment and alleviate poverty for smallholder farmers in impoverished countries. To learn more about TREES, visit http://trees.org/.